crashing waves

Crashing Waves is a work of fiction. Any
references to people, places, or events, are
products of the author's imagination.

Copyright @ 2021 by Jenna Rose

Artwork, interior and cover design by Jenna Rose

All rights reserved, including the right to
reproduce this book or portions thereof in any form.

2021 First Edition @ Jenna Rose

Rose, Jenna, author, artist
Crashing Waves | Jenna Rose

For information about special discounts
for bulk purchases, for schools, mental health
organizations, bookclubs, etc
please contact author directly.

Meditations
Issued in Print and Electronic formats.

IBSN 978-1-7779240-0-3
IBSN (ebook) 978-1-7779240-1-0

crashing waves

meditations to set yourself free

jenna rose

published 2021
toronto

a letter to the reader:

may this book be a companion to you through the highs and lows of being human. may it be the thread that ties your human body to your infinite soul. may it be the meeting point of the timed and the timeless. may it ease the hard days, and witness the glory days.

in the midst of pain, loneliness, and the heartache of being human, in the moments of beauty and love, in the easy times and the hard times, in the calm, the storm, the light, the waves, may this book be a reminder to you, that you are free.

with love,
jenna rose

for my love

art slows us down
allows life to enter us

jenna rose

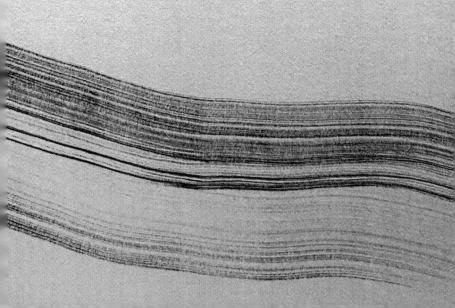

calm

jenna rose

i want to hide
and be seen
all at once

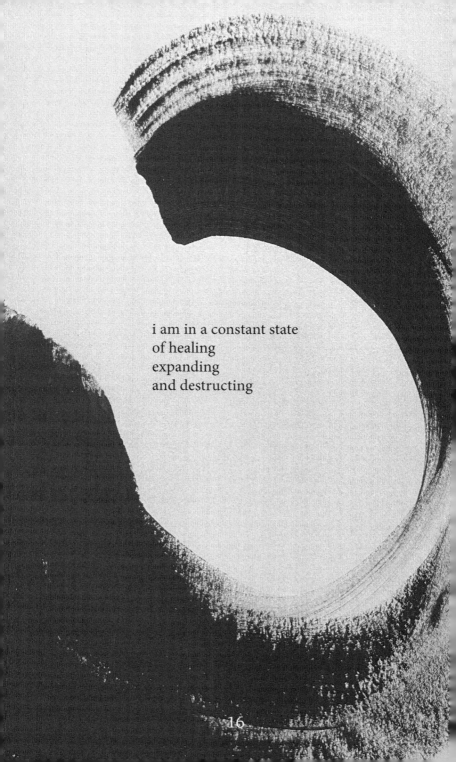

i am in a constant state
of healing
expanding
and destructing

jenna rose

one earth
hurtling through eternity
together

crashing waves

my life is made up
of half finished things
half finished art
and half finished
stories with strangers

jenna rose

i am so lost
and so alone

what if in the end
i am nothing more
than mediocre
what if all i've
ached for
broken and bent for
is forgotten
what if my one true love
leaves
will it all be worth it
if in the end
its just me

jenna rose

its exhausting
working my movements
and words
every attempt
to avoid
pain

fear makes my legs turn numb
steals the words off my tongue

love does the same

jenna rose

i sit in the quiet
alone
and whisper your name

crashing waves

sometimes my heart
and my mind
feel like lost loves
come undone
with no way back

jenna rose

darkness my old friend
back so soon?

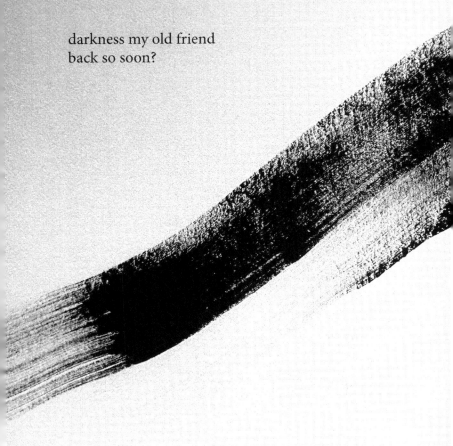

i twist and turn
but i can't escape
this anxious body

jenna rose

i am the caller
you are the called
i want to be like you

but instead i will call you
again
and as it rings
i will think about how
you never call me drunk

i made so many attempts
to disguise my vulnerability

jenna rose

i wish i had been busy learning
how to flourish in it

only
in the slowed
space of stillness
can you hear
heartache
sing through the cracks
of your body

jenna rose

everything makes me think of you

my precious heart
i will be your keeper

crashing waves

we belong to each other
the torn and the tearing
the addict
the fix
too bad to stay
too good to leave

i tried to make you mine
pulled you from the ground
like a flower
i should have known
something so beautiful
wouldn't last long
in a tiny cup
of water

you are hard to describe
your soul is so big

crashing waves

i wanted to be loved by you so bad
i forgot everything else i wanted

jenna rose

maybe
maybe
so many fucking
maybes

i ask you for your words of wisdom
on how to write

you smile and say

keep it simple
just the bones
and the beauty

rw.

jenna rose

sometimes
i wish the word tomorrow
was never invented

crashing waves

i only write because i know the ache
of loss and loneliness

jenna rose

and i know the medicine is in the beauty of it

your desires are not your own
they are answers
to the world's call
entrusted
to you
your assignment
this one
precious
lifetime

jenna rose

if i no longer have blocks
or reasons why not
no gatekeepers in my way
no complaints
no pains and aches
no battle to be fought
no jailer
no jail
no drama
no chase
no wrong doers
or hell to pay
if there is no antagonist in my story
if these wars are nothing more
than a dream
if my existence has been built upon
what i am against
who am i
when the thing i have spent
my precious time hating
is gone

in the fall
goodbyes are the hardest
gravity whispers til eyes
give up their tears
smile and gut punch
a cliff of goodbyes
smiles turned cries
i used to cry
but i dont anymore
i'm better now
and now when you leave
i ache
but only because its the fall
cold
quiet
and fleeting

i ask you to kiss me
and when you lean in
i turn away

i give you my mind
my time
my best jokes
but your attention
seems only granted to me when
i give you my body

nobody looks anybody
in the eyes too long
you either break your heart
or fall in love

i call you back to bed
as the lake calls me
to her shore

jenna rose

i just wanna makeout like the old days

crashing waves

your breath is captured summer breeze

your touch made me feel
like i hadn't eaten
in days

you were perfect medicine
for me and my lonely soul

jenna rose

i spent so many hours on you

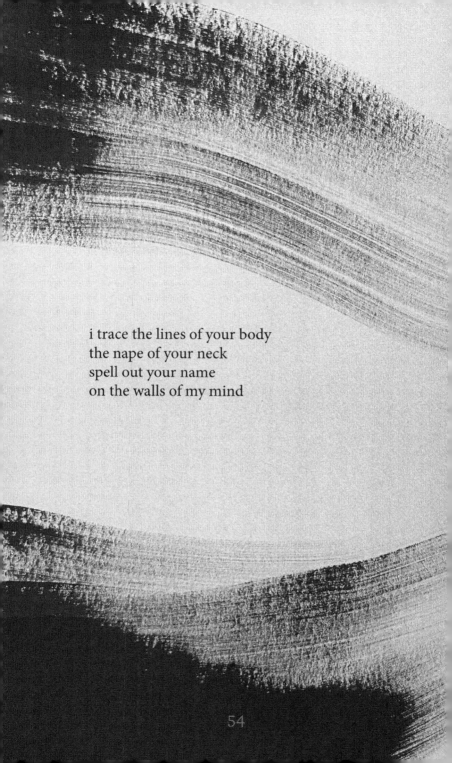

i trace the lines of your body
the nape of your neck
spell out your name
on the walls of my mind

jenna rose

life is getting sick
over and over again
and searching
over and over
for the cure

crashing waves

what prisons have i called home?

jenna rose

it is an exhilarating thing
to tell the truth

i get so drunk on wanting
i can't see straight
walking through paradise

jenna rose

i am surrounded by excess
yet i still crave something more

crashing waves

hidden deep
inside my perfectionism
is a fear of failure
of rejection

jenna rose

be grateful for the dark times
they make for great art

storm

tell me

when did you love yourself the most?

jenna rose

you can build up walls
place
all
the
pieces
perfectly
sturdy
and
certain
but
then
one
tiny
misstep
and the home you thought was foolproof

tumbles

crashing waves

you didn't believe me
when i told you i went to bed alone
or that we spoke
no more than four words
*yes i was drinking but i am telling you the truth i
got into that small bed by myself*
the words fall out of my mouth
with nowhere to land
i tell you that i didn't know
who was behind me
when i woke up
just warmth
and danger
pressed into me
your eyes made me feel like a liar
like my pants weren't really at my knees
like i hadn't woken up to a stranger inside me
you didnt use the word rape
you questioned and questioned
then whispered

he said you wanted it

jenna rose

a new kind of emptiness filled me

crashing waves

hate
grew
in
my
heart

jenna rose

like a good soldier
fear got to work
building walls around me

crashing waves

and the night sky
was painted a different
shade of dark
after that

jenna rose

there is no road map
no how to books
on recovering the parts of yourself
that were stolen
no podcasts or affirmations or therapies
that could make you feel whole
no amount of drinks or sleep or showering
that could obliterate
you from me
its like being dropped
in a foreign land
with no way home

crashing waves

the waves would come
the sun would keep
painting the days yellow
the flowers would smile and flicker
but i always
carried a little bit of sadness
with me

i've gotten good
at becoming so still
and small
every inch of my body collaborating
in a tiny silent symphony
to survive

sometimes the darkness is startling
it comes blazing through your eyes
in the mirror
sometimes it slips in the door behind a
comment from your lover or mother or friend
sometimes it sends hate shooting through you
like lightning
sometimes it is too tired to come shooting
so it steals you away under the covers,
searching for the cure in your sleep
sometimes it feeds you poison
and sometimes it doesn't feed you at all
sometimes it is whipping and cracking
sometimes it is slow and searing
some mornings it greets you first thing,
awaiting the moment your mind returns to
this place and time
sometimes it can't wait til morning

but one thing that remains the same
our visits are easier when i give darkness
a warm welcome

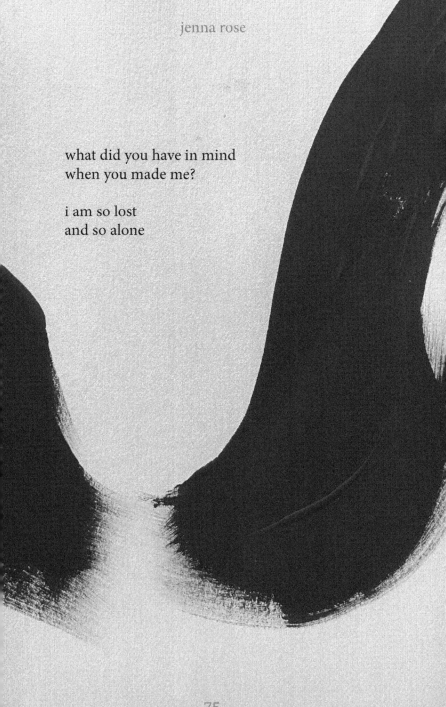

what did you have in mind
when you made me?

i am so lost
and so alone

alone

the word stings my insides

jenna rose

seeking
wanting
this is where art finds you

in the depths of loneliness

crashing waves

withheld your love
your praise
rationed it
tiny doses
just to keep me coming back
to your empty well

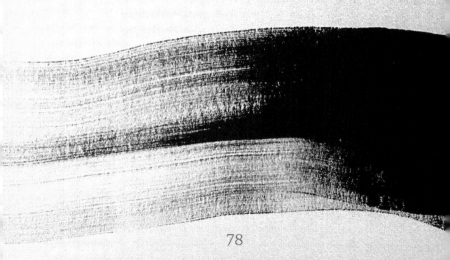

it seems i am not enough
not liked enough
charming
enough
beautiful and funny enough
not successful enough
accomplished enough
i am not the best
or strongest
or calmest
i dont know
much about anything
or what i will become
i dont know
what will ever be
enough
to make me
worthy of
even
liking
myself

i would cling to the littlest
whisp
of love
make something out of nothing
so i could eat
feast
on air

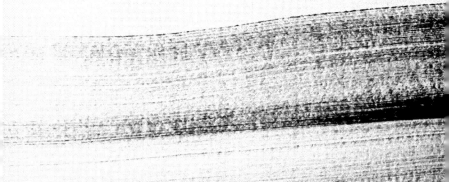

jenna rose

i look at the one i hurt
and hate myself more than enough
for the both of us

crashing waves

i always planned on leaving
leaving
turned to staying
and i find myself
here
staring into nothing
wishing it was something

jenna rose

gambling on you
again and again

i wanted you to crave me
thirst for me
but you had feasted
you didnt need me

even the wildest storm
the angriest tyrant
the cruelest illness
is seeking
to be witnessed

crashing waves

i want to be unwavering
certain and promised
but i am just human
fickle and foolish

i walk from the house
to the lake
and back
but reasons follow me everywhere
reminding me why
i can't

sometimes i wonder if god
or whoever put me here
made some sort of mistake
the wrong time or the wrong place
forgot a few
key
ingredients
sometimes this feeling is fleeting
and sometimes it is days before i can wring
it out of my clothes
sometimes
its a long time
before i remember
that god doesn't make mistakes

jenna rose

where has my wild gone?

i want to be a lover
i want to promise you forever
as the moment slips into nothingness
i want to churn your shame
into freedom as you
pour your secrets into me
in your cruelest moments
i want to soften for you
i want to surrender my sanity
in pursuit of this love

jenna rose

slide over to your edge
meet the place
where magic is born

crashing waves

i came here to meet
the furthest corners of myself
to stay when my bones want to run
to steal moments
alchemize loneliness into power
jealousy into fuel
i came to touch every texture of the earth
and feel sound dance through my blood
i came to fill my clothes with the smell of
campfires
and drink coffee naked at noon
to get my medicine straight from the ocean
and trade my hail mary's for sex
i came to understand love
in distance and silence
and feel spirit in my mother's chest
to know freedom in tight spaces
in the realm of fear
i came for love

jenna rose

don't let that burning in your belly
go to waste
we need to rebuild
more than you
need to calm down
set this place on fire

crashing waves

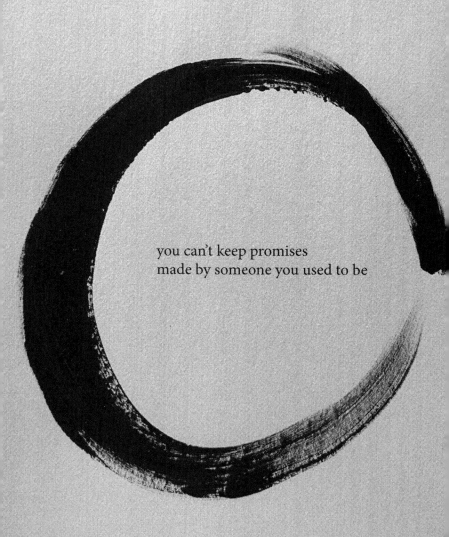

you can't keep promises
made by someone you used to be

jenna rose

i have broken my own back
and heart
trying to appease you
please you
with my smallness
as if my existing
was a threat to your livelihood
as if
my roar
would drown out yours
we didn't learn how to howl for eachother
we learned
humble
obedience
so the starving pack wouldn't turn
and eat us
i guess that is the result of hunger
salivating
over one bit of
meat

light

it may sting some eyes
shining your light
in a room that has been dark for so long

jenna rose

i am learning how to fold into myself
like the lake does
at her shore
over and over

crashing waves

you can't invite your dreams in
if there's nowhere for them to sit

jenna rose

the world outside
is sleeping
i look down at my body
rising and falling
in perfect time
and see
the ocean

crashing waves

i sit with my fear
my longing
my jealousy
my hate
talk truth to the mirror
and tell her
my darling,
i'm not going anywhere

jenna rose

the details of you
tasted like sweet berries

your smile makes my body sing
in places i didn't know existed

i see you
   and the parts of me i thought were dying
are flooded with life

there is nothing casual
about this existence
there is no promise
of tomorrow's and next time's
the only certainty
is the preciousness of this
right here
moment

jenna rose

fill the torture rooms of your mind
with laughter
unchain the prisoners
let the bad guys off this time
lift the window open
and let the breeze carry in
a new day

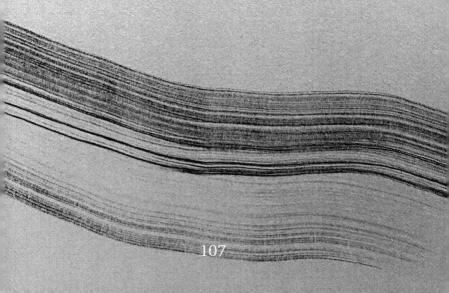

crashing waves

you only get years, days
fleeting moments

don't cheat yourself of it

your story is unique
and everywhere
you soften
and the world softens too
you open
and the world folds into you

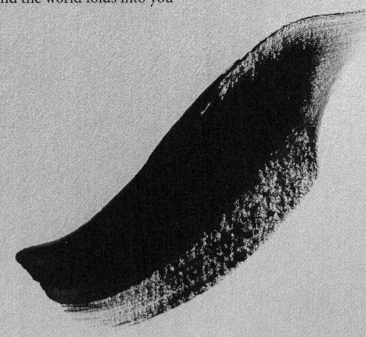

crashing waves

let love be a welcome stranger
let the breeze soften your pace
let romance make your stomach drop
and your hands reach for something to hold
let the simple words in a song
make your chest swoon
let the wild push and pull of life
beckon you fuller and deeper into your truth
lie on the ground
and let the line that separates you
and the magic of this place
dissolve

jenna rose

there are paths in the light
and paths in the dark
my footprints can be found
in the mud
of both

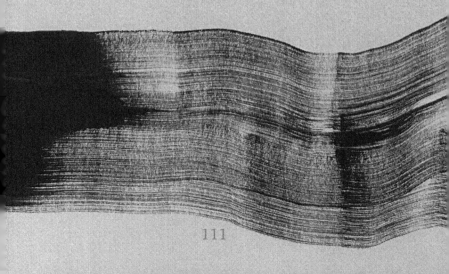

crashing waves

i have no more time
for seeking
waiting
for wisdom to fall on me
i ask
simple and clean
and am flooded
in my answer

too many times
i have said yes when i mean no
i have said
no thank you
while my body screamed
yes
i have hidden
what asked to be shown
and waited
for what passed me by
i have watered
my
self
down
and now
i'm gonna give it to you
straight

your world is pulsing with richness
beating
throbbing
aching
for you to notice
beautiful
simple
and changing

drop yourself
for a moment

jenna rose

no one was at the beach
just me and the lake
i laid on the ground as close as i could get
and asked
how are you so strong?
she said
know when to be still
and know when to come crashing

crashing waves

inside the room
it is dark and quiet
just the heart beating steady for me
the breath moving in and out without me
asking
blood travelling endlessly
wanting nothing in return
my feet touch the floor again
as if by no choice at all
and the soul who has been hiding
opens her eyes

i run
from the shower
to the table
dripping water
on the hardwood floors
scratching out this
fleeting
idea
that could be brilliant
or useless
it is not for me to decide
for me
my duty is
only
to drip water
on the hardwood floors

crashing waves

your touch
is much more than
hands and lips and hips
against mine
its a transfusion
barreling life
into every river of blood
coursing through my body

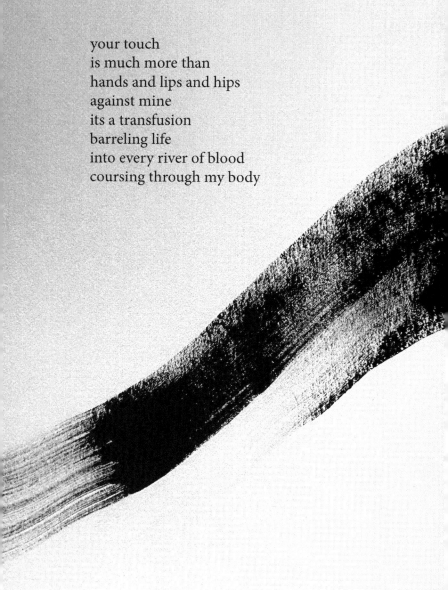

jenna rose

i love the process
of becoming one
with you

crashing waves

you are the shape of joy

do you really think
the one who gave us
all this
the warmth
the water
the food
the sex
the one who made everything we see
put us here
to suffer?

speak like your words are a gift
like the letters falling out of your mouth
will adorn your listener more beautifully
than any fine jewels
like the words are not words but the sonnet of
your soul
like every sentence
is drawing you closer than cell mates
sentenced to life
like your words are dessert
like you are god's hired translator
like you have only minutes left of this
borrowed time to tell it exactly how
beautiful it is
like you drank truth serum for breakfast
like you are sharing the password to nirvana
and the word love is tattooed down your spine
like your words are the secret recipe for bliss
like grace is your native tongue
and your life is a promise made between
something more and the moment slipping
past

your existing is proof
the world has more than enough space
to hold the vastness of you

crashing waves

up late writing love letters to the new me

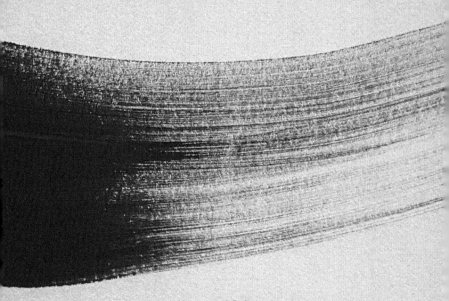

jenna rose

all my best tricks
to pull her closer

crashing waves

you ask me to choose
left or right
right or wrong
but how can i decide
when i am the sum
of all the parts

jenna rose

i will not fall
into the delusion of
us and them
we are too much of the same soul
to be mistaken
that my beauty is not within them
and their darkness
not in me

the sun
drips down my cheeks
and i remember
for a moment
i am not alone

jenna rose

you have been loyal to logic
and sanity
long enough
let your dreams
take flight

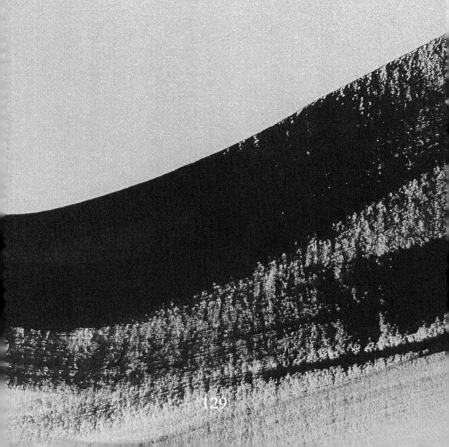

touching you is delicate
a classified conversation with god
i choose my words carefully
slow dancing my fingertips
across your body

jenna rose

there is no one
too smart
too small
too bigoted
too beautiful
too intimidating
too dissimilar
to sit
and have tea with

suspended
in the space between
awake
and asleep
i find myself
i find us

jenna rose

you gave your body to me
made it a home
my great welcoming
your blood
became my blood
your bones
my bones
mother
the only power
great enough to
pull
me
from
bliss
into this thick
fast
world
the great prophet
the giver
of life's
boundless
desire

keep going
there are versions of you
awaiting
your arrival

you are the answer
you are magic
divinity
embodied
you
are the one
most capable of holding the depth and beauty
of you
you are brilliant
just look at you
you are a russian doll of gifts
you are so worthy
of being seen
through loving eyes

crashing waves

leap baby
leap

waves

jenna rose

we dance the same
slow and smooth
back and forth
me
and the
waves

crashing waves

last night
i cut my hair
i dreamt of wolves
and a tap that ran gold
i went straight to the lake
in the morning
the breeze kissed me
til my clothes fell off
and the lake pulled me in
i let the cold make new
every cell in my body
let
every
extra
thought
dissipate
and let the wild
find her way back home

jenna rose

there are stories inside me
that i don't know
are true or false
weaved out of need
or bent into shape from pain
there are stories
i've carried for so long
i don't remember
when i picked them up
and had forgotten that
i can put them down

life has changed you
shaped you
your eyes
carved
beautiful and honest

jenna rose

i want to flower and fruit for you

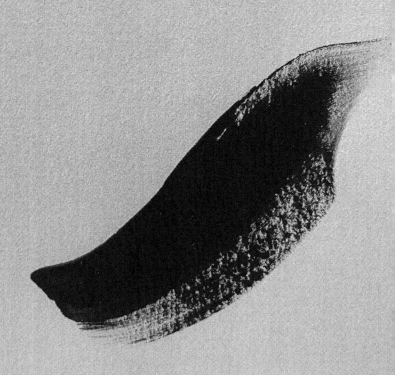

plump and gushing
like mulberries

i need silence
rich
full
silence
and space
space that has not been self paparazzied to a pulp
space that has not been eroded by addiction
heckled by the future
gnawed by the past
space that sifts effortlessly
from passion to softness
space that is occupied
only by bodies
space that smells of olden days
and passes slow like summer in the 60s
slow
full of wanting and waiting
just questions
no answers
just easy walking
back in time
space that consists of less
matter
and more
in between

your life drenched in love
is the greatest act
of rebellion

stop waiting in smallness
for the right moment
to burst you into being
you are the only one
you have been
waiting for

do not look to the greats
to fill your cup
to ring the bells of wonder
and stir the ideas latent in your mind
do not wait in praise and adoration
or flock at the foot of pedestals or gurus
do not rely on their light to guide you
through your own path
do not squander the discoveries
the creations
the art
the beauty
the romance
the groundbreaking potentialities
that are hibernating inside you
your existence is a portal
the instructions have been tucked away
in your own pockets from the very beginning
you arrived in this place and time
with everything you need
already
inside you

jenna rose

no more comparing
no more complaining
my need for freedom is too great

crashing waves

let the colours bleed
let the sun adorn your body
in gold
find the hidden beat
that leads your entrance
they came to see you
let the truth be
the final
word

jenna rose

i don't want to be scholarly
or polished
i want to come undone
lie naked in the sand
feel only the warm breeze and your kiss
on my head
reduced to the warmth
of the thin space
between our sun drenched bodies

crashing waves

there will always be suffering
there will be pain and brutality
cages and rulers
tyrants and lawless laws
there will be unjust acts
heartbreaking acts
ruthless
unfathomable
insidious
acts
there will be corruption
and war
division and fear
hate will find a way to go on

there will be a bottomless pit of reasons
this world could break your spirit

go on with love anyways

my darling
my sweetheart
lent to me from the heavens
let us make love and laughter
of all this borrowed time

crashing waves

have you seen the side of a cliff
where the dynamite has built roads
and the layers of changed earth
are out on display?
i want to see you that way
i want to see the artistry of time on your soul
i want to crack you open
and marvel at the way life has shaped you

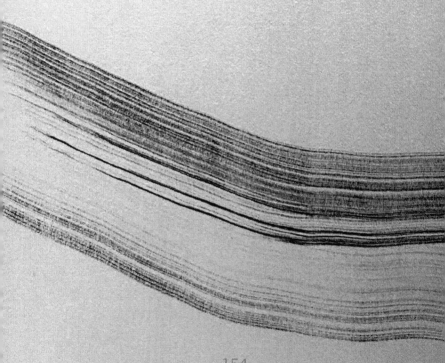

jenna rose

your skin
smells of new life
and eternity
all at once

look around
you're in the right place
there is a stage
below your feet
calling to you

you are right on time

jenna rose

like wine i have been
basking
aging
preparing
for your lips
the finest thing you have ever
tasted

do not smoulder your burning desire
for something more
or cover your mouth
when your soul cries in betrayal
do not fall for the smooth talk
of indifference
or settle
into cheap
loveless
days
for the sake of safety
give your word
that you will love
you will love what you love without shame
you will lose yourself in the company
of the ones who lavish in your spirit
you will unfold into pleasure
and abandon all sense of have to's and
supposed to be's
you will give your life up
to the docket of your soul
we have only
a little while

jenna rose

these cracks inside
are valleys
tectonic plates
shifted
pieces of ourselves
broken
apart
let the wind and waters pervade every channel
let the rivers run deep and wide
let the space between
far and close
be filled
with love

crashing waves

when love leaves
let the hollow channels
remind me
i have loved deeply

despite loss and heartbreak
i will leave my door open
so happiness can stop by
for no reason at all

i am too vast
too broad
too wild
too much
like trying to catch a waterfall
just holding out a cup

jenna rose

light the match of your soul
with a life lived at the edge
where the chance of falling is great
but the chance of feeling truly alive
is greater

a power more limitless than you can fathom
created everything
and is capable
of creating
your deepest desires

jenna rose

i am made up of pieces
pieces you wouldn't think could fit together
just right
pieces of before
and after
pieces of my mother
and my father
pieces of all the places i've been
and all the lovers i've tasted
i am made of pieces
that shouldn't fit together
but do

crashing waves

in the end
we must all say goodbye
lose everything
leave alone
as we came
whole
and
fleeting

jenna rose

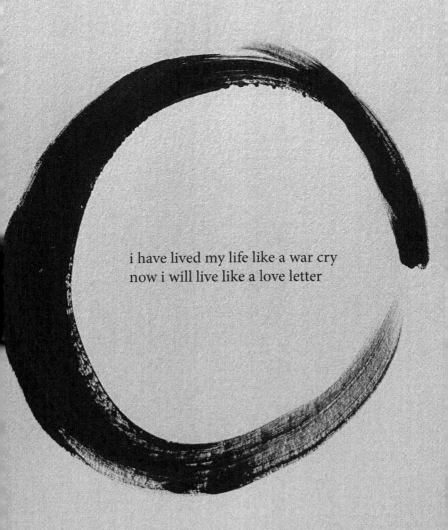

i have lived my life like a war cry
now i will live like a love letter

crashing waves

the wider you open the window
the more light can pour in

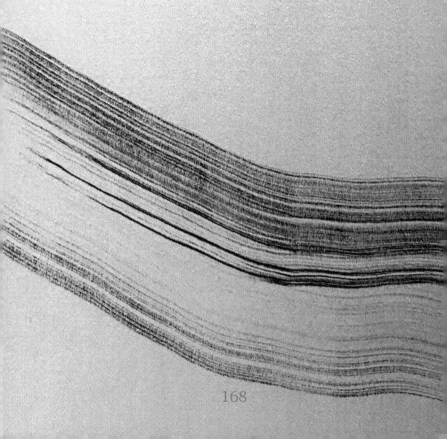

jenna rose

i will not be better later
i won't be neater in my home
or in the way i eat
i won't be funnier or more desirable
i wont be skinnier or prettier
fancier or fitter
i won't be more well read
or more refined
i will not be any better
there are no improvements
to be made
no mending or preparing
no fixing
no changing
there is nothing
wrong
so when my dreams
come knocking
it will be me
as i am
welcoming them
at the door

crashing waves

let the stories of tomorrow
forget my name
leave it written
in the hearts
of the ones i love

i wonder now
if love is loud
if it must preach its holy word
if it must come booming
if it must be bold and certain
i wonder now
if in the quiet
when all the noise
and all the busyness
has retired
if there
in the stillness
is the voice of love

jenna rose

i knew finally
as i looked out at the
crashing waves
tilted my head back
breathed out
i am yours

writing
art
interior + cover design

by

jenna rose

about the writer

jenna rose is a writer, artist and actor, currently living by the lake in toronto, canada. her mission is to live as freely and honestly as possible, and inspire others to fall in love with their humanness, their spirit, and their infinitely beautiful selves.

when she is not writing, painting or in film, she enjoys gathering one of a kind fashion and design pieces, tending to her inner landscape, and sipping coffee by the lake while listening to good music.

she sees life as an endless series of opportunities to expand and set yourself free by living as close to your truth as possible.

you can find more of her work at
jennarose.online + ig @jennarosebc

write to set yourself free

Manufactured by Amazon.ca
Bolton, ON